JOHN GARDNER

A Burns Sequence

Op. 213

VOCAL SCORE

Music Department
OXFORD UNIVERSITY PRESS
Oxford and New York

Oxford University Press, Walton Street, Oxford OX2 6DP, England
Oxford University Press Inc., 200 Madison Avenue, New York, NY 10016, USA

Oxford is a trade mark of Oxford University Press

© Oxford University Press 1995

All rights reserved. Apart from any fair dealing for the purposes of research or private study, or criticism or review, as permitted under the Copyright, Designs and Patents Act, 1988, this publication may only be reproduced, stored, or transmitted, in any form or by any means, with the prior permission in writing of Oxford University Press.

Permission to perform the work in public (except in the course of divine worship) should normally be obtained from the Performing Right Society Ltd. (PRS), 29/33 Berners Street, London W1P 4AA, or its affiliated Societies in each country throughout the world, unless the owner or the occupier of the premises being used holds a licence from the Society.

Permission to make a recording must be obtained in advance from the Mechanical Copyright Protection Society Ltd. (MCPS), Elgar House, 41 Streatham High Road, London SW16 1ER, or its affiliated Societies in each country throughout the world.

780.44 GAR
3 180 373 792

CONTENTS

		Page
1	Prayer under the pressure of violent anguish	1
2	Raging Fortune	7
3	My luve is like a red, red rose	10
4	Will ye go to the Indies, my Mary?	15
5	O whistle an' I'll come to you	20
6	Ca' the yowes to the knowes	27
7	McPherson's farewell	33
8	Paraphrase of the First Psalm	43

This work was commissioned by the British Federation of Young Choirs with funds provided by the Arts Council of England, and first performed by combined BFYC choirs and the Scottish Chamber Orchestra, conducted by Christopher Bell, in City Hall, Glasgow on 12 March 1995.

Orchestration:
2 flutes (2nd doubling piccolo)   timpani
2 oboes   1 percussion: side drum
2 clarinets (2nd doubling bass clarinet)   triangle
2 bassoons   cymbals
2 horns   glockenspiel
1 trumpet   strings
3 trombones

Duration: about 25 minutes

Conducting scores and orchestral parts are available on hire

Composer's note:

Though of peasant origin, Burns was a highly cultured man: vastly well-read and with a knowledge of foreign languages, mathematics, and music. He cut a striking figure amongst the *cognoscenti* of Edinburgh society.

This sequence contains poems to do with some of the many varied activities which exercised his fancy during his short life. His religious conviction (in the hymns which begin and end the work); his *penchant* for writing new words to traditional Scottish melodies (in 2 to 7); his delight in both romantic love (in nos. 3 and 4) and philandering (in no. 5); and his not infrequent use of High English rather than the Lallans with which he is usually associated (in nos. 1, 2, and 8).

He made two versions of *Ca' the yowes* (no. 6), being later dissatisfied with his first attempt to match this wonderful tune. Nevertheless I have used his earlier version which, though less 'literary' and less 'romantic' than its successor, has, I feel, more passion. This is the only traditional melody I have used, apart from an altered version of the Slow March *McPherson's Lament* in no. 7, which sets a poem telling the stirring tale of the freebooter who played the fiddle at his public execution in the marketplace of Banff in 1700.

John Gardner

1. Prayer under the pressure of violent anguish

O Thou great Being! what thou art,
    Surpasses me to know;
Yet sure I am, that known to Thee
    Are all Thy works below.

Thy creature here before Thee stands,
    All wretched and distrest;
Yet sure those ills that wring my soul
    Obey Thy high behest.

Sure Thou, Almighty, canst not act
    From cruelty or wrath!
O, free my weary eyes from tears,
    Or close them fast in death!

But, if I must afflicted be
    To suit some wise design!
Then man my soul with firm resolves
    To bear and not repine!

2. Raging Fortune

O, raging Fortune's withering blast
    Has laid my leaf full low!
O, raging Fortune's withering blast
    Has laid my leaf full low!

My stem was fair, my bud was green,
    My blossom sweet did blow;
The dew fell fresh; the sun rose mild,
    And made my branches grow.

But luckless Fortune's northern storms
    Laid a'[1] my blossoms low!
But luckless Fortune's northern storms
    Laid a' my blossoms low!

[1] a' = all

3. My luve is like a red, red rose

O, my luve is like a red, red rose,
    That's newly sprung in June.
O, my luve is like the melodie,
    That's sweetly play'd in tune.–

As fair art thou, my bonie lass,
    So deep in luve am I,
And I will love thee still, my dear,
    Till a' the seas gang[2] dry.–

Till a' the seas gang dry, my dear,
    And the rocks melt wi' the sun!
And I will luve thee still, my dear,
    While the sands o' life shall run.–

And fare-thee-weel,[3] my only luve!
    And fare-thee-weel a while!
And I will come again, my luve,
    Tho' it were ten thousand mile!

[2] gang = go
[3] weel = well

4. Will ye go to the Indies, my Mary?

Will ye go to the Indies, my Mary,
    And leave auld[4] Scotia's shore?
Will ye go to the Indies, my Mary,
    Across th' Atlantic roar?

O, sweet grows the lime, and the orange,
    And the apple on the pine;
But a' the charms o' the Indies
    Can never equal thine.

I hae[5] sworn by the Heavens to my Mary,
    I hae sworn by the Heavens to be true,
And sae[6] may the Heavens forget me,
    When I forget my vow!

O, plight me your faith, my Mary,
    And plight me your lily-white hand!
O, plight me your faith, my Mary,
    Before I leave Scotia's strand!

We hae plighted our troth, my Mary,
    In mutual affection to join;
And curst be the cause that shall part us!
    The hour and the moment o' time!

[4] auld = old
[5] hae = have
[6] sae = so

5. O whistle an' I'll come to you

O whistle an' I'll come to ye, my lad!
O whistle an' I'll come to ye, my lad!
Tho' father an' mither an' a' should gae[7] mad,
O whistle an' I'll come to ye, my lad.

But warily tent[8] when ye come to court me,
And come nae unless the back-yett[9] be a-jee;[10]
Syne[11] up the back-style and let naebody see,
    And come as ye were na[12] comin' to me.–
       O whistle &c.

At kirk, or at market, whene'er ye meet me,
Gang by me as tho' that ye car'd na a flie;
But steal me a blink o' your bonie black e'e,[13]
    Yet look as ye were na lookin' to me.–
       O whistle &c.

Ay vow and protest that ye care na for me,
And whyles[14] ye may lightly my beauty, a wee;[15]
But court not anither tho' jokin' ye be,
    For fear that she wyle[16] your fancy frae[17] me.–
       O whistle &c.

[7] gae = go
[8] warily tent = take care
[9] yett = gate
[10] ajee = ajar
[11] syne = then
[12] na = not
[13] e'e = eye
[14] whyles = sometimes
[15] a wee = a little
[16] wyle = lure
[17] frae = from

6. Ca' the yowes to the knowes

Ca' the yowes[18] to the knowes,[19]
Ca' them where the heather grows,
Ca' them where the burnie[20] rowes,[21]
My bonie dearie!

As I gaed[22] down the water-side,
There I met my shepherd lad:
He row'd[23] me sweetly in his plaid,
An he ca'd me his dearie.

Ye sall get gowns and ribbons meet,
Cauf-leather shoon upon your feet,
And in your arms I'll lie and sleep,
An' ye sall be my dearie.

If ye'll but stand to what you've said,
I'se gang wi' thee, my shepherd lad,
And ye may row me in your plaid,
And I sall be your dearie.

While waters wimple[24] to the sea,
While day blinks in the lift[25] sae hie,
Till clay-cauld death sall blin' my e'e,
I sall be your dearie.

Ca' the yowes to the knowes,
Ca' them where the heather grows,
Ca' them where the burnie rowes,
My bonie dearie!

[18] yowes = ewes
[19] knowes = hillocks
[20] burnie = stream
[21] rowes = runs
[22] gaed = went
[23] row'd = wrapped
[24] wimple = meander
[25] lift = sky

7. McPherson's farewell

Sae rantingly,[26] sae wantonly,
   Sae dauntingly gae'd he,
He play'd a spring,[27] and danc'd it round
   Below the gallows-tree.

Farewell, ye dungeons dark and strong,
   The wretch's destinie!
McPherson's time will not be long
   On yonder gallows-tree.

O what is death but parting breath?
On many a bloody plain
I've dared his face, and in this place
I scorn him yet again!

Untie these bands from off my hands,
   And bring me to my sword;
And there's no a man in all Scotland,
   But I'll brave him at a word

I've liv'd a life of sturt[28] and strife;
   I die by treacherie:
It burns my heart I must depart,
   And not avenged be.

Now farewell light, thou sunshine bright,
   And all beneath the sky!
May coward shame distain his name,
   The wretch that dares not die!
Sae rantingly &c.

[26] rant = lively tune
[27] spring = lively dance
[28] sturt = contention

8. Paraphrase of the First Psalm

The man, in life where-ever plac'd,
   Hath happiness in store,
Who walks not in the wicked's way
   Nor learns their guilty lore.

Nor from the seat of scornful pride
   Casts forth his eyes abroad,
But with humility and awe
   Still walks before his God.

That man shall flourish like the trees,
   Which by the streamlets grow:
The fruitful top is spread on high,
   And firm the root below.

But he, whose blossom buds in guilt,
   Shall to the ground be cast,
And, like the rootless stubble, tost
   Before the sweeping blast.

For why? that God the good adore,
   Hath giv'n them peace and rest,
But hath decreed that wicked men
   Shall ne'er be truly blest.

for Harry McNab of Glasgow, fifty years a friend

A Burns Sequence

Robert Burns John Gardner
Op. 213

1. Prayer under the pressure of violent anguish

© Oxford University Press 1995   Printed in Great Britain

OXFORD UNIVERSITY PRESS, MUSIC DEPARTMENT, WALTON STREET, OXFORD OX2 6DP
Photocopying this copyright material is ILLEGAL.

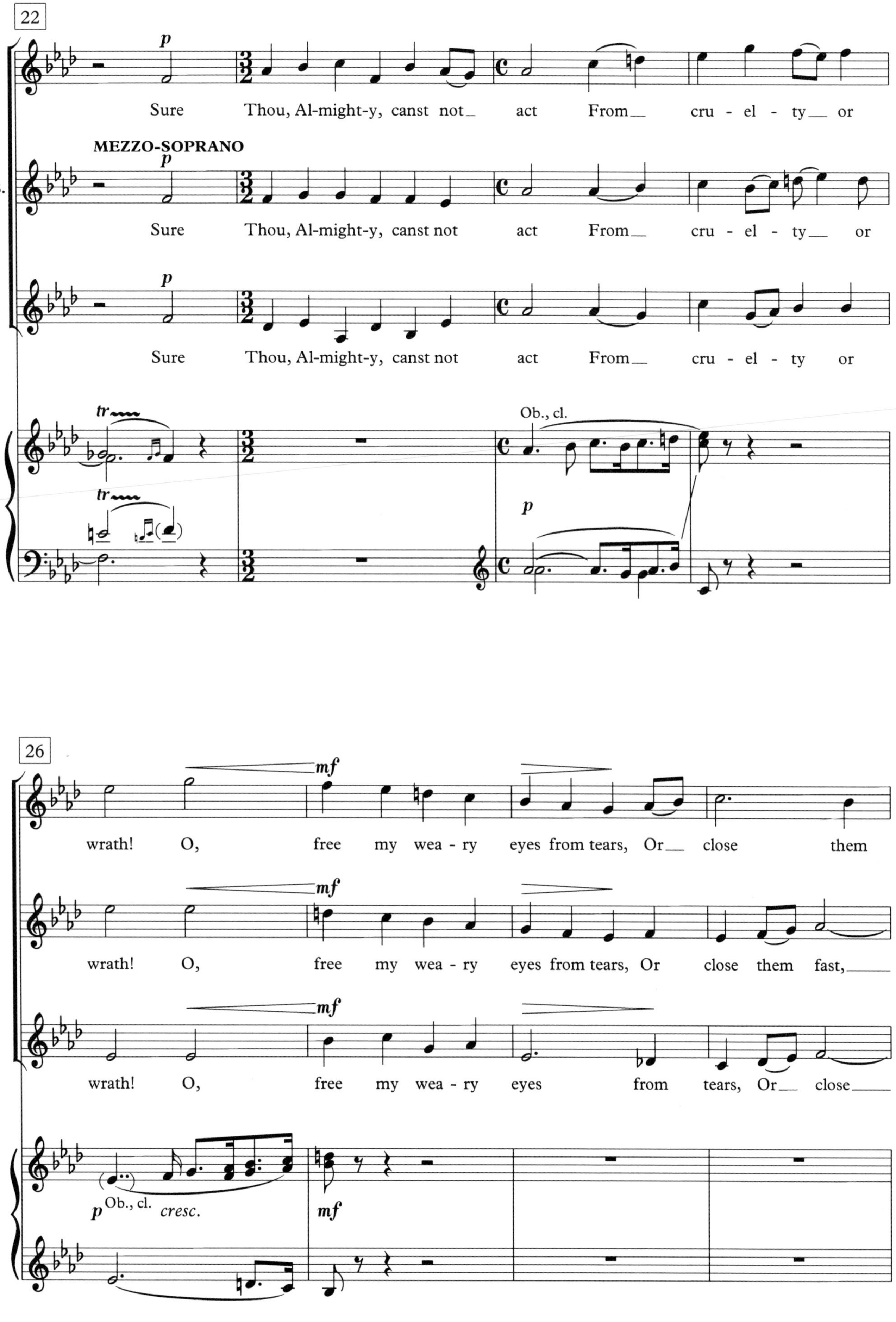
22
S.
p
Sure Thou, Al-might-y, canst not_ act From_ cru - el - ty_ or
MEZZO-SOPRANO
M.S.
p
Sure Thou, Al-might-y, canst not act From_ cru - el - ty_ or
A.
p
Sure Thou, Al-might-y, canst not act From_ cru - el - ty or
tr
Ob., cl.
p
26
mf
wrath! O, free my wea - ry eyes from tears, Or_ close them
wrath! O, free my wea - ry eyes from tears, Or close them fast,
wrath! O, free my wea - ry eyes from tears, Or_ close_
p Ob., cl. cresc.
mf

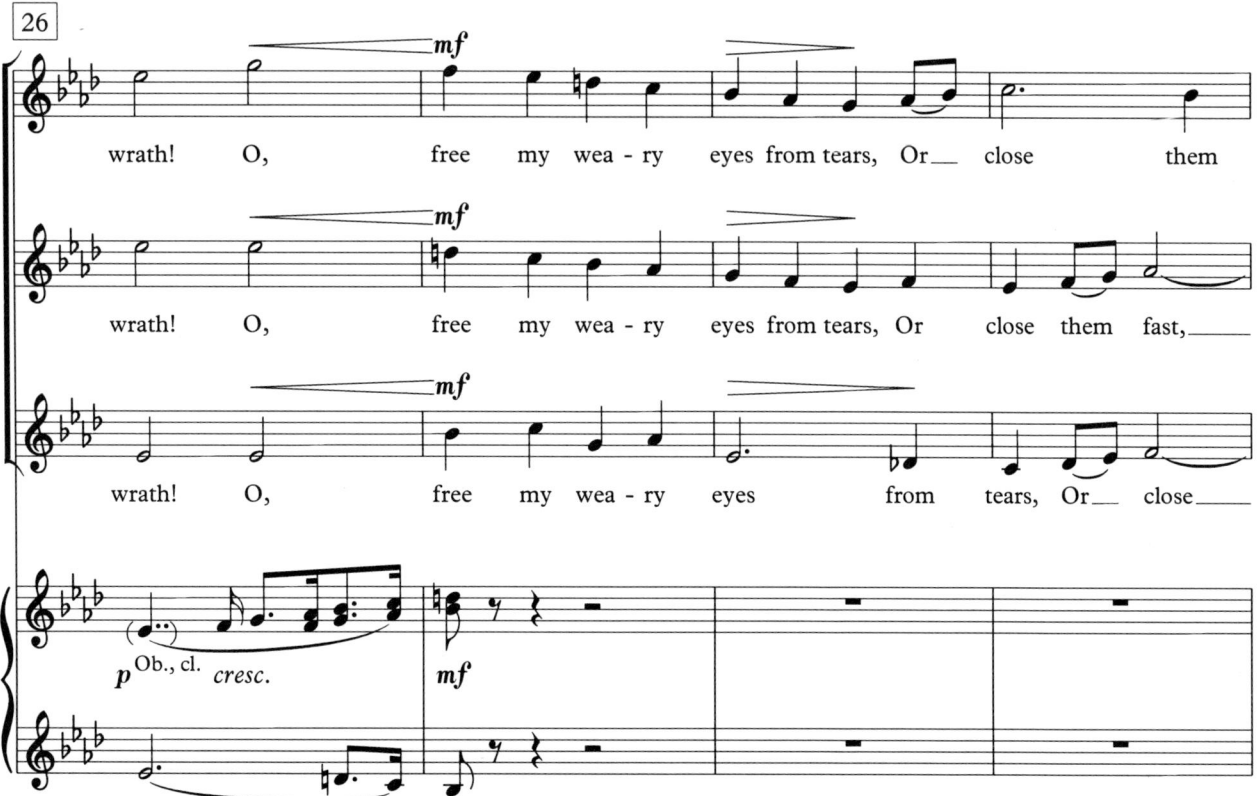

2. Raging Fortune

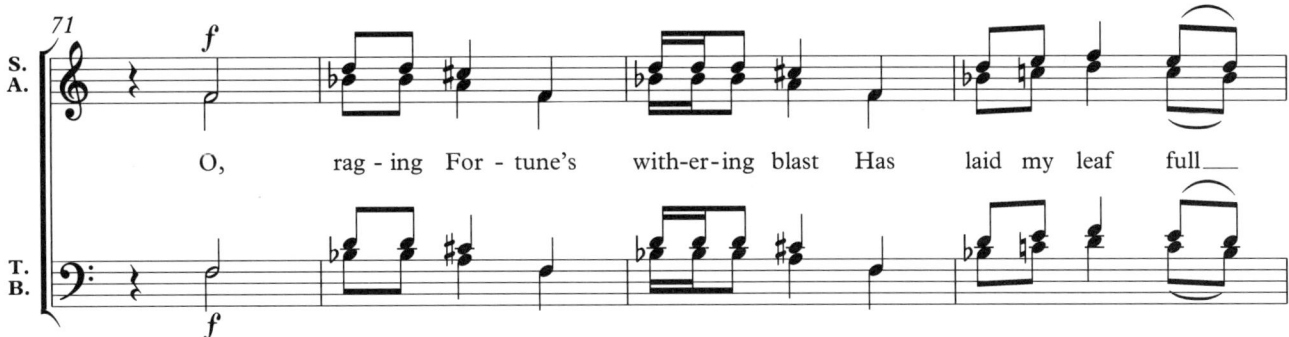

* Bracketed passages should only be played if the chorus can't otherwise pitch it's entries.

3. My luve is like a red, red rose

4. Will ye go to the Indies, my Mary?

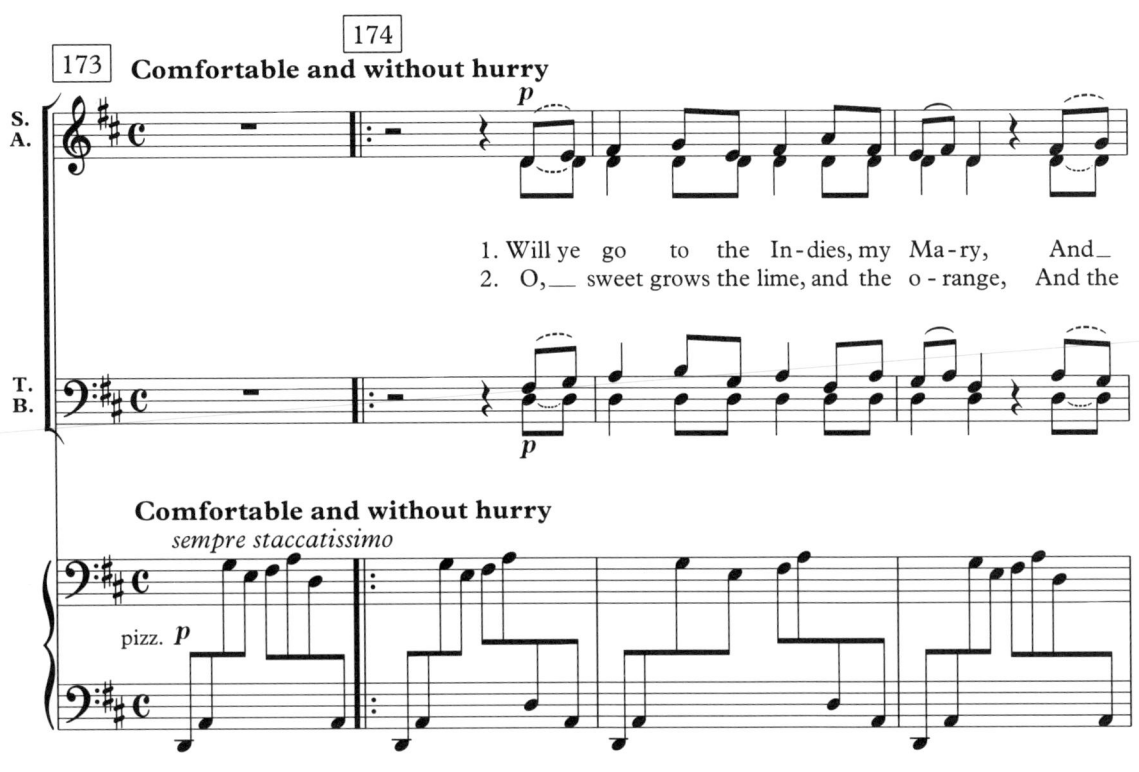
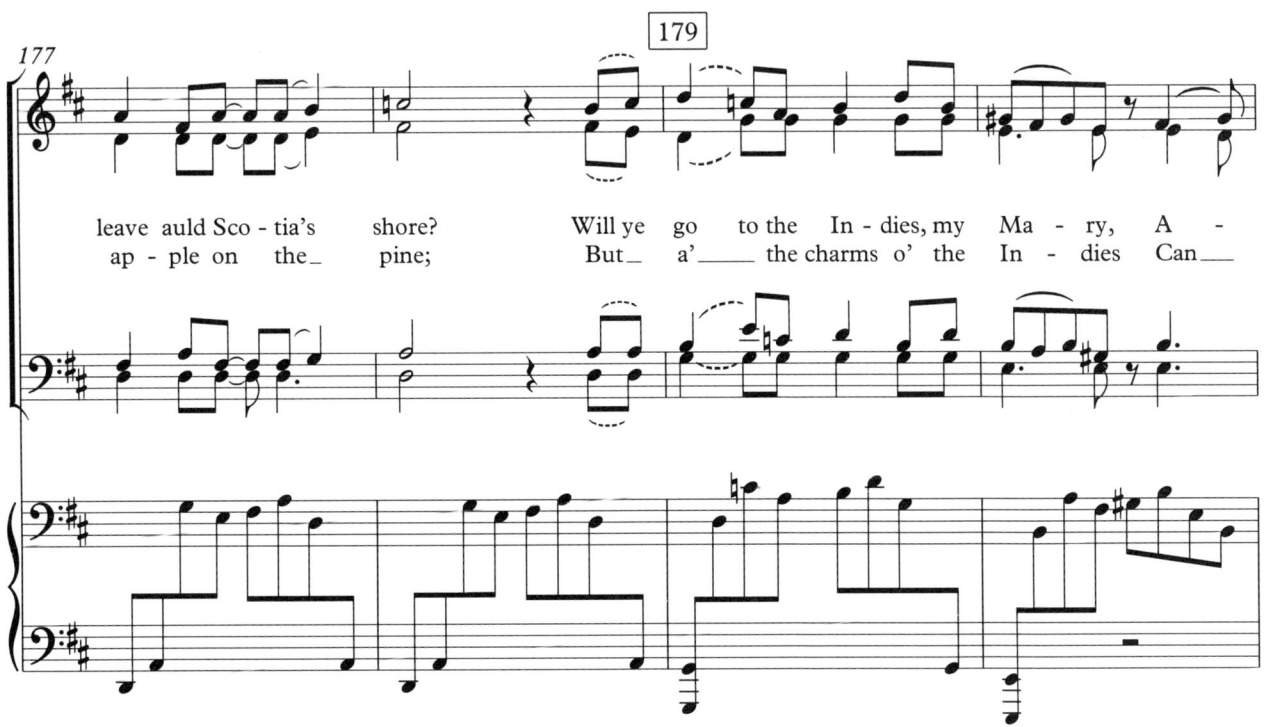

5. O whistle an' I'll come to you

* The men either sing or whistle; there must be no mixture.

6. Ca' the yowes to the knowes

Ca' the yowes to the knowes, Ca' them where the hea-ther grows, Ca' them where the burn-ie rowes, My bo-nie dear - ie!

As I gaed down the wa - ter-side,

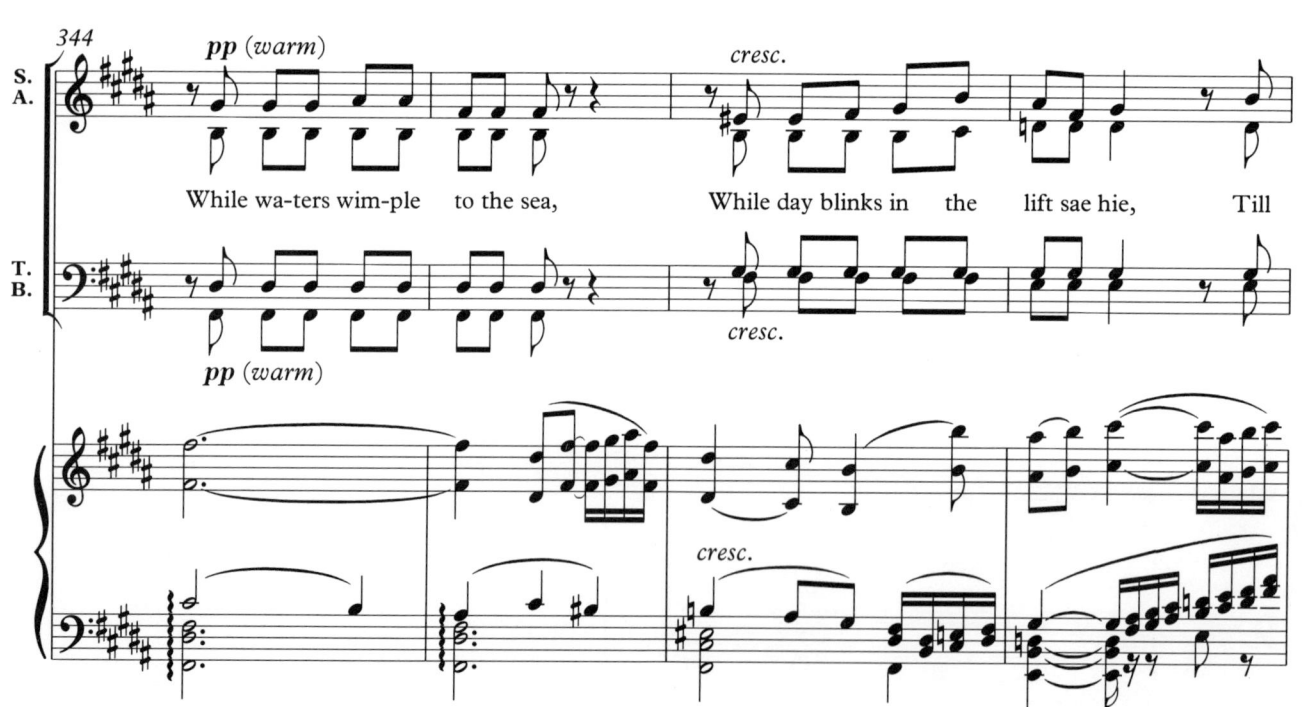

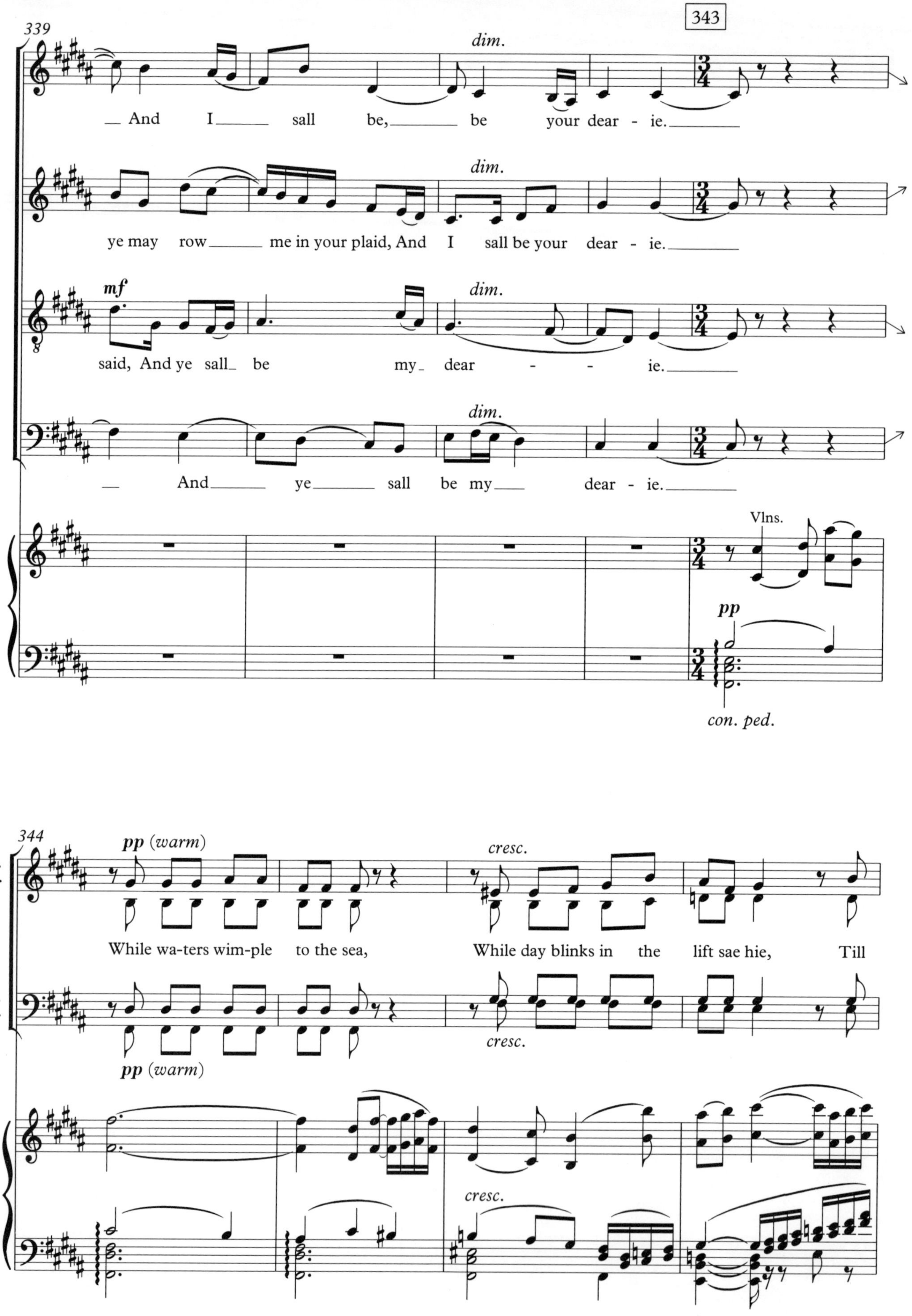
339
343
dim.
And I sall be, be your dear - ie.
dim.
ye may row me in your plaid, And I sall be your dear - ie.
mf
dim.
said, And ye sall be my dear - - ie.
dim.
And ye sall be my dear - ie.
Vlns.
pp
con. ped.
344
pp (warm)
S.
A.
cresc.
While wa-ters wim-ple to the sea, While day blinks in the lift sae hie, Till
T.
B.
cresc.
pp (warm)
cresc.

clay-cauld death sall blin' my e'e,
Ye sall be my dear-ie.'
I sall be your dear-ie.'

Ca' the yowes to the knowes,

Ca' them where the hea-ther grows, Ca' them where the burn-ie rowes,

My bo-nie dear - - ie!

7. McPherson's farewell

Slowish march (crotchet beat)

Snare drum
dim. poco a poco

liltingly
Solo Vln.

flirtatious and coy

S. Sae_ rant-ing-ly, sae wan-ton-ly, Sae daunt-ing-ly gaed he, He__ play'd a spring, and danc'd it round Be-

A.

- low the gal-lows - tree.

Fare - well, ye dun-geons dark and strong, The wre-tch's des - ti - nie! Mc - Pher-son's time will not be long On yon-der gal-lows - tree. O what is death but part-ing breath? On ma-ny a blood-y plain I've dared his face, and in this place I scorn him yet a - gain!

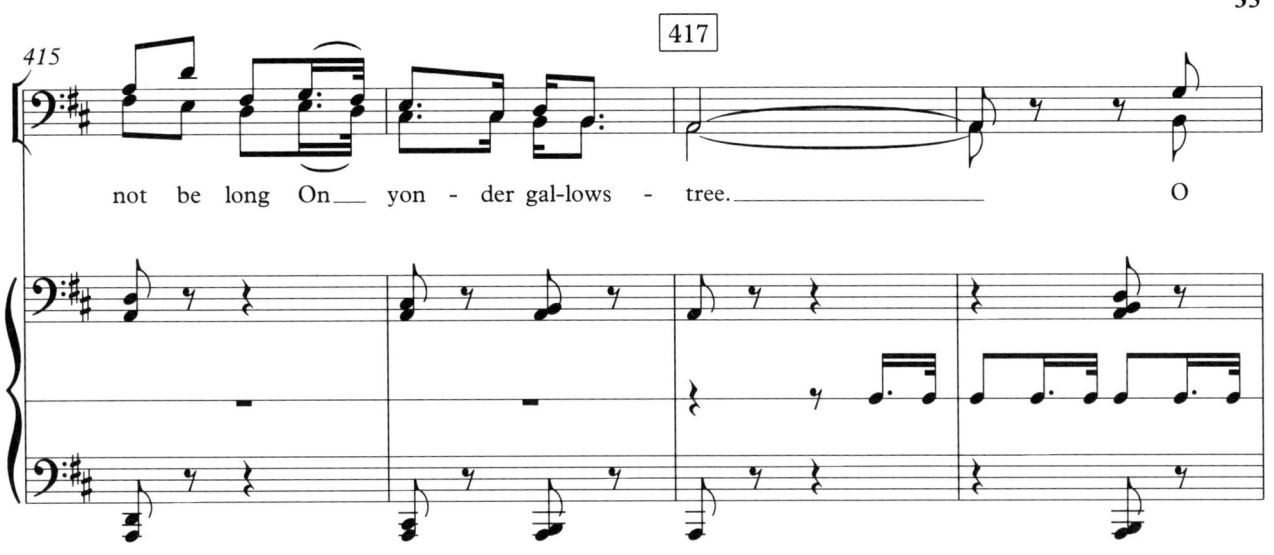

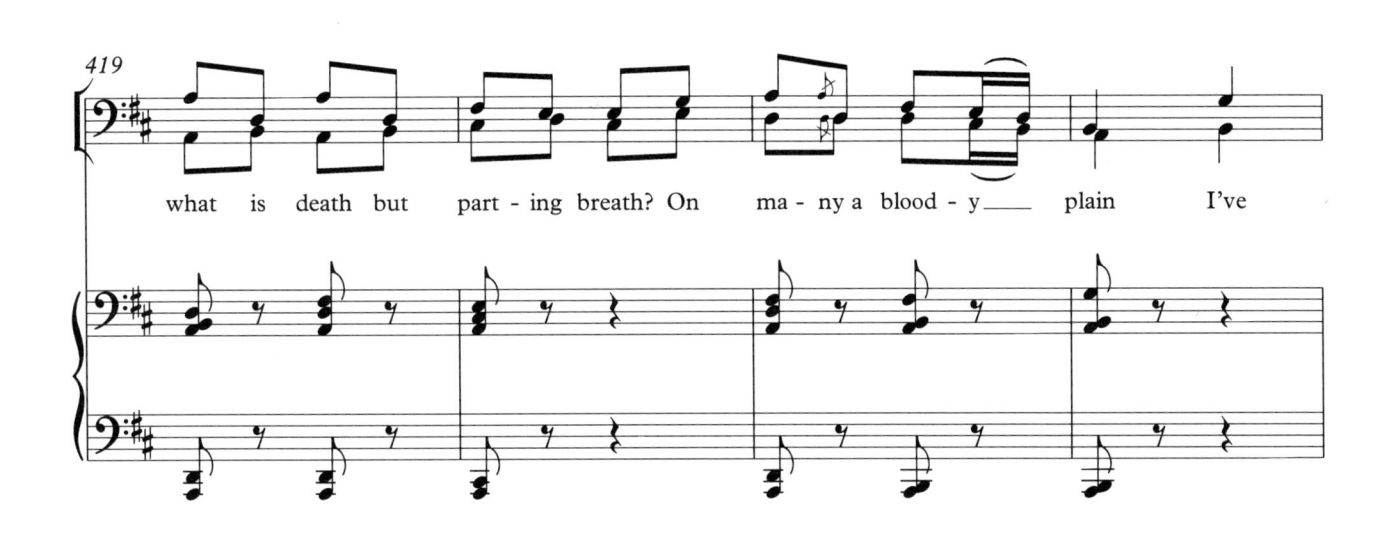

Un-tie these bands from off my hands, And bring to me my sword; And there's no a man in all Scot-land, But I'll brave him at a word.

Sae rant-ing-ly, sae wan-ton-ly, Sae daunt-ing-ly gaed he, He play'd a spring, and danc'd it round Be-low the gal-lows-tree.

S: I've liv'd a life of sturt and strife; I die by treacherie: It burns my heart I must depart, And

A: I've liv'd a life of sturt and strife; I die by treacherie: It burns my heart I must depart, And

T: I've liv'd a life of sturt and strife; I die by treacherie: It burns my heart I must depart, And

B: I've liv'd a life of sturt and strife; I die by treacherie: It burns my heart I must depart, And not a-ven-ged, not a-ven-ged be.

not a-ven-ged, not a-ven-ged be.

not a-ven-ged, not a-ven-ged be.

not a-ven-ged, not a-ven-ged be.

Now

Now

Now

Now

fare - well light, thou sun-shine bright, And all be-neath the sky! May

cow-ard shame dis - tain his name, The wretch that dare not die!

41

S.

A.

Sae___

rant-ing-ly, sae wan-ton-ly, Sae daunt-ing-ly gaed he; He play'd a spring, and danc'd it round Be-low the gal-lows-tree.

Solo Vln.
pp

dim. al niente

8. Paraphrase of the First Psalm

The_ man, in life wher - e - ver_ plac'd, Hath hap - pi -

-ness in store, Who walks not in the wick-ed's way Nor learns their guilt-y lore.

Nor from the seat of scornful pride Casts forth his eyes abroad,

But with hu-mi-li-ty and awe Still walks be-fore his God.

That man shall flour-ish like the trees, Which by the stream-lets grow: The fruit-ful top is

That man shall flour-ish like the trees, Which by the stream-lets grow: The fruit-ful top is

That man shall flour-ish like the trees, Which by the stream-lets grow: The fruit-ful top is

That man shall flour-ish like the trees, Which by the stream-lets grow: The fruit-ful top is spread on___ high, And firm__ the___ root be - low.___

spread on___ high, And firm__ the___ root_ be - low.___

spread on___ high, And firm the___ root be - low.___

spread on high, And firm the__ root be - low.___

But_ he, whose

But he, whose

blos - som buds in guilt, Shall to the ground be

blos - som buds in guilt, Shall to the ground be

And, like the root-less stub-ble, tost Be-fore the

And, like the root-less stub-ble, tost Be-fore the

cast,

cast,

sweep-ing blast.

sweep-ing blast.

For why? that God the good a-dore, Hath giv'n them

For why? that God the good a-dore, Hath giv'n them

For why? that God the good a-dore, Hath giv'n them

For why? that God the good a-dore, Hath giv'n them

peace and rest, But hath decreed that wicked men Shall ne'er be truly blest, ne'er tru- ly blest.

ne'er tru- ly blest.

ne'er tru- ly blest.

ne'er tru- ly blest.

poco più mosso

stringendo

rall. *mf cresc.*

Shall ne'er

Shall ne'er

Shall ne'er

Shall ne'er

Ewell, Christmas Eve 1993

Music origination by Barnes Music Engraving Ltd., East Sussex
Printed in Great Britain by Halstan & Co. Ltd., Amersham, Bucks.